EARTH
BOUND

COMPANIONS

Earth Bound Companions
Poems by William Hershaw
Art by Les McConnell

Published by Grace Note Publications
Scotland, 2021

ISBN: 978-1-913162-15-3

EARTH BOUND

COMPANIONS

Poems by William Hershaw
Art by Les McConnell

Earth Bound Companions

I first worked with the Kinghorn artist Les McConnell on *The Sair Road*, published by Grace Note Publications in 2018. The book was my attempt to portray the religious story of *The Stations of the Cross* in the context of the Fife mining community I grew up in and to show how the miners and their families tried to save their jobs and look after each other through times of strife. In the book, Jesus was depicted as a communist miner. Publisher Gonzalo Mazzei suggested that the text would be enhanced with illustrations. The published hardback book was a wonderful production and contained Les' stark and memorable black and white drawings on facing pages to the Scots Language poems as well as his "striking" jacket cover. The original drawings, now framed with the aid of a grant from Fife Council, became part of The Hewers of Coal and Verse Exhibition held at the Lochgelly Centre in the summer of 2018 to mark the fiftieth anniversary of the death of Fife playwright Joe Corrie. That Autumn the exhibition travelled over the Forth Bridge and was put on display at The Scottish Poetry Library in Edinburgh. The pictures were captured also in Frieda Morrison's film The Sair Road which featured interviews with Les and I sitting on a bench at Lochore Meadows: <https://www.scotsradio.com/the-sair-road/>. They have now found a permanent and appropriate home on display at the Corrie Centre in Cardenden.

The artistic collaboration with Les worked a treat. The method was a simple one. I gave Les the poems to read without comment and he produced the images. These were far more than illustrations, although they fulfilled this remit with ease, but rather were interpretations and translations and extrapolations. New works of art that emerged when text transformed into visual images.Their power derived not just from Les' skill in multi-media presentation but in his ability to choose and arrange telling symbols in a way that caught the soul of the poems and their message.

We were both keen to continue this creative partnership but wondered if it was destined to be a one off. Would it work for other subjects in different contexts? I have long been interested in writing poems in Scots about animals. In 2015 I had written a sequence titled *Buirds* which was published as a limited edition pamphlet by the Dumfries prize winning publisher and acclaimed artist Hugh Bryden. The pamphlet included lino cuts of the different birds by ornithologist and artist Fiona Morton and Hugh designed the production to include a pop up eagle that spread its wings and "flew" when you opened the book. An exhibition of Hugh and Fiona's work with the poems was exhibited in 2016 at the St Andrews Preservation Trust Museum as part of the Stanza Poetry Festival.

Around this time I read primatologist Frans De Waal's book The *Bonobo and the Atheist*. This book suited my anthropomorphic temperament. Based on his studies over many years of two of our closest relatives, chimpanzees and bonobos, De Waal put forward a research and evidence based argument that these species have a sense of fairness and morality. He discusses the implication that ethics and particulary empathy and compassion may be the result of biology rather than religion. Rightly or wrongly I found it heartening to believe that the imperative drive of evolution may not be simply the survival of the fittest but a progression toward kindness and mindfulness to other beings (whether we believe in God or not). At a time when so many species, including our own, face imminent future extinction I was glad to know that we have much in common with some of our Earth bound companions, to use the famous words of Robert Burns from his poem *To A Mouse*. Maybe it is not so wrong to imagine our animal neighbours in our own likeness as a means toward understanding our commonality as well as our differences? De Waal proved conclusively that the animals he studied often made deliberate choices that disadvantaged themselves in order to help their fellow primates. Some of our politicians have not evolved so far.

This collection started out under the working title of *Bowff! A Scots Baistery* and I thought of it as an illustrated book to begin with. Detailed applications were sent off for a grant to assist with publication costs but nothing was forthcoming. That was a blow and made me question the validity of the project. Still, I started to send draft poems to Les and astonishing pictures would come back via email with the animals brought to life, often in unexpected situations. Some of these were sent to Ian Moir, the curator of the Fire Station Creative Gallery in Dunfermline. It was agreed with Ian that we would put on an exhibition titled *Earth Bound Companions* through the month of March in 2020. Ian gave us lots of sound advice and put us on to Veronica and her picture framers in East Calder. We wanted big white frames that were large enough to contain Les' paintings mounted plus the text of the poem: viewers would get a two for one experience and see at a glance how the art and the poetry were related. True to form, *Earth Bound Companions* quickly shape-shifted into other interesting forms as we went along. I write mostly in Scots because Scots is mainly misunderstood and neglected and needs the attention. But a number of poems started to get written in English and it seemed right to leave them be - it's a fine enough language after all. Other poems appeared that were not about specific animals, that were about fabled animals or in one case an animal that no one has ever seen. Poems emanated that were to do with sentience rather than baisties. Then there was one about Bert Jansch but we both liked it. Neither Les nor I have ever been too rules driven - the whole point of our partnership is the artistic freedom we have to do as we like. My collaborator began a stunning new series of big paintings based on Shakespeare plays. This was a reversal of the text-first practice and I found it difficult to do what he had been doing with ease all along - initially I ended up providing Scots translations of Shakespeare's English.

And so to the night of the big launch. It was a great night, a packed Gallery with so many old friends and familiar faces in attendance and beautiful live music from Jenn Knussen on harp and Erik Knussen on cello to set the mood. The reaction to the 27 chosen works on display was hugely positive. To quote the artist, the exhibition was about to go viral. Even as I was making my introduction speech there was speculation of an imminent lockdown and sadly the Fire Station Gallery had to be closed within a week or so due to the spread of the terrible Covid Epidemic. The Gallery itself would remain closed during the summer with our work still adorning the walls but sadly, with the floor space empty and nobody there to see it and read it.

All of this is a roundabout way of explaining the purpose of this pamphlet put together by our friend Gonzalo Mazzei. It's a retrospective of an exhibition that was short and sweet. If you didn't make it then this is the next best thing. It's not comprehensive - it's too big a task to knock on the doors of all those who bought a painting and ask permission to take a photograph (most of the works found a good home to go to). Hopefully it provides a flavour of what the exhibition was all about and is a fitting memento of a happy time and a great night. We have also taken the chance to continue what is still a work in progress by including new additions to the baistery. *Ainster Herbour Hogmanay*, allows us to pay homage to John Alexander's work of genius *Tight Squeeze*. At some point we hope to get back to another happy time at the Fire Station in the future with our friends. But that will be with a new venture. Watch this space. If you are interested in what we have been doing during Lockdown check out *Saul Vaigers*, our book of Scottish saints and a companion volume to this, also published by Grace Note Publications.

William Hershaw

Earth Bound Companions Exhibition
Poems by William Hershaw
Art by Les McConnell
Curated by Ian Moir

Fire Station Creative, Carnegie Drive, Dunfermline
3rd – 29th March, 2020:

Original inventory and order of exhibits:

1. *Haggi*; **2.** *Angie*; **3.** *William Turner's Rain Steam Speed*; **4.** *Moth Larva In The Great Tapestry*; **5.** *Urban Tod;* **6.** *Badger;* **7.** *Earth Bound Companions;* **8.** *Basking Shark;* **9.** *The Futtock;* **10.** *Nessie;* **11.** *Artificial Intelligence;* **12.** *A Resident Blackbird Speaks;* **13.** *Ravens;* **14.** *Grey Heron;* **15.** *Le Jourre de Guitarre by Picasso;* **16.** *The Castle Baist;* **17.** *A Midsummer Night's Dream, Act 5, Scene 1*; **18.** *Macbeth, Act 5, Scene 5;* **19.** *King Lear, Act 5, Scene 3;* **20.** *Hamlet, Act 2, Scene 2;* **21.** *Romeo and Juliet, The Prologue;* **22.** *The Tempest, Act 1, Scene 2: (Ariel's Sang)*; **23.** *Shakespeare in Glencoe: (Macbeth, Act 1, Scene 4)*; **24.** *Straundit;* **25.** *Roe Deer Fawn;* **26.** *Unicorn;* **27.** *Ghosts*

Exhibition

Exhibition

Les McConnell,
Frieda Morrison &
William Hershaw, L to R

Earth Bound Companions
Book Edition

Contents

Earth Bound Companions

Hauf-droukit baist, I amnae blate or feart -
Ye hunker doun aside me mang the stibble -
Ma whuskers sense a kind but bruckle hairt
That wadnae wish me herm or unco trouble.

Wanrestit baist, you're trummlin like a lintie,
And you're ower fou - wi guilt and worry thrang.
Like aa your kind, you bicker, boast sae vauntie -
You think mice daft, their smaa lives ower fore lang.

Sair-hoasting baist, happed in a threid-bare coat -
Bide in the Here and Nou's contentit state,
Ging lown, fearnae the futret, baudrons, stoat -
Gey suin eneuch you'll flee wi taloned Fate.

Ocht - Silly Man, o futures drear ye tell!
Greet nae for me, greet anely for yersel.

Urban Tod

Tak a swatch at me nou! I'm sae citified I run
Ma ain taxi business at weekends:
Ma fares are ower peeved tae ken I'm a tod.
I drive drunks tae their last trains, tak
Bare-buffed quines tae clubs and cocktail dens,
Hen-pairties and fluffy pink bunny lugs
Succumb tae auld siller fox's chairms.
I ken ilka short cut and rottan run
And hae the odd brush wi the City authorities.

I mak a guid leivin, though it's no ma first walin.
And when the strung-out junkie muin
Nid -nods ower in the wee smaa hours,
I bring hame a takeaway.
"It maist be a michty fine toun, Dad!"
The bairns aa yelp when I smoul hame.

Moth Larva In The Great Tapestry

History I digest slawly:
Hou it sticks in ma thrapple!
I got masel taigelt amang the Stuarts,
Coudnae follae the threid through
The Reformation, swallaed the Union haill
Till it unraivelled in thrums.

I bide in the past and hae collogued
In monie a fine stitch-up
In the deid o nicht in Parliament Haa.
I play ma fou pairt in Life's rich pageant:
Eggs liggit in the past pupate,
Predestined tae unfankle Fate.

HENRY VIII
ACT OF SUPREMACY
1534

REFORMATION

CHARLES I

JAMES VI & I

MARTIN LUTHER 1517

Straundit

We are haulin oursels up a beach,
Wi ilka wave, wi ilka jaup, again and again.
Some o us hae raxt tae the fuithills o the dunes,
Ithers are speldert, seawaur on the wane,
Or juist skailing back doun the drains
And runnels that scour the weet saund.
There's chiels ill-taen that a fortunate swaw
Heezes their rivals an unwaured gain.
Ane fae the stert fleed ower faur, ower fast –
He's rizzert, his shell's juist a fossil stain.
Aye three steps faurrit and syne twaa back,
Molluscs schauchling, an undeemous chain.
Be kittle! Be quick! Be soupple! Be swick!
Gin ye howp tae win or even remain
In the race, wi the drave in the muin-cawed tide,
Tae staund straucht in the sun, like Gods.
We are haulin oursel up the beach,
Wi ilka wave, wi ilka swaw, again and again.

Ravens

Thought and Memory
Unwelcome smartass double act
Are out on tour again
Patrolling the daily battlefield,
Practising physical comedy
In the gossipy wind.
Croaking their black humour,
Sarcastic one liners,
From dented roadside crash barriers.
Beady-eyeing you up for the next pratfall.
Bad news, these two.

A Resident Blackbird Speaks

They come in the months up to March
Escaping the cold in the East.
Hard grafters, I'll give them that much,
Filling their parasitical bellies
With our insects and British berries.
They never stop.
Chirps and tweets on the left wing insist
We're all the same. Maybe
From a distance we all look like birds.
But this lot bring their own songs with them,
Their beaks not tawny orange but black,
There's no golden circlet round the eye.
If one comes near my nest I'll see him off.
There should be controls on where they fly.

William Turner's Rain Steam Speed

A minor detail, this long-lugged thing?
A hare taking form in the oils,
Behind it pechts an arthritic train.
Ploughman and boatman are left behind
But not the hare ahead of its time,
But not the hare that leaps the line
With driving thighs pivoting its hip wheel.
An arcing and stretching of bones,
Bent to its limit in a forced fix,
It feels a frozen nape of fear
From the firebox breath encroaching.
Its futures swirl in a stationary moment, see,
It's frozen there, fleet-footing it from death,
Avoiding the glaring eye willing it down,
Avoiding the ground opening all around
Yet somehow always bounding ahead
Of the linear lie, the unending race,
The thirling of progress, time and space.

Badger

I'm the Very Reverend Maister Brock,
Dug-collared, deckit-out in seemly sabbath bleck.
I pad about the pairish wi houlet eyebrows
Heezed at gauns-on, houghmaghandis,
Wanton Sabbath brekkin amang futret schemies.
Whiles Papish mowdiewarps and English shrews
Skitter and chitter anent their diet o worms,
I delve in the airth wi ma neb,
Tae grolloch up oubits that faa ma wey.
Ma manse is biggit gey swack on a glebe
O strang and deep-delvit scriptural foundations,
Haes monie chaumers but nae potpourri.
Ancient and justified, I'm blythe and joco
Gnawing at teuch-ruitit theological pirns.
A richtous elected brock, I've smaa sympathy
For they sinfou craturs tint in the wuids.
Aa ma teeth are provided for.

Basking Shark

Like a hippy Para Handy
Coming doun caller and lown fae the heichs
O a braw blaw o Gulf Stream plankton,
I yawned and breeched, hinging aff Aultbea,
Transmitting guid vibes tae Mither Gaia.
Syne – Ouyahboyserr! An oar in the ribs.
Tak tent whaur you're gaun, lang man!
I'd heard tell o monsters like him.
See hou he's evolved, wi his rod and his biro
That mak siccar o his survival!
He thirls leivin craturs in his poems,
Clauchts us aa in a jyle o his words.
The ark o the baists are forfochten by him:
The swag-bellied cou, the beer-bellied puddock,
The auld blin cuddie and the donnert deuk,
Etherised sauls enjambed in his fell bleck buik.
Keep your Darwin, I'd raither hae Creationism.

The Futtock

I've aye been here in plen sicht
aa alang, yet nae aabody can see me.
At onie gien time
aiblins a hunner maun catch a glisk.
I'm comely, brawsome and byordinar.
Ye wadnae ken, though ye've stuid closehaund,
and goaved intil ma een,
felt the flauchter o ma saul,
the trummle o ma bruckle hert,
athout recognition.

Indigenous, a pairt o me's in
ilka atom o this kintrae:
common as tatties and herring,
oorie as a broch that haps the muin,
hodden grey as a nellyphant,
kenspeckle as a crocodile,
douce as a pouter dou,
unco as a wicht -
catch me unawaurs, ettle tae thirl,
and I'll birl and tak your airm aff.

Aiblins ane o thir days you'll lairn
a veison straucht and gleg.
You'll see me haill for whit I am.
Betimes I'm bidin on a new-mintit state
that's worth me botherin tae kyth in.

Reporting Scotland

Relentless the roadkill
Counted on your crooked road,
You hang their carcasses nightly on our screens.
Endless your litany of negatives.
In Scotland today only:
Murder, rape, accident, death,
Failure, allegation and sleekit attack.
So what that a bairn laughed on a Lewis swing,
A Dundee man allowed his neighbour
To win at dominoes,
A woman from Methil escaped from Hell
Graduating with first class honours?
You presume to edit our day,
Let nothing good be heard,
As if you laundered out the clean
Leaving only stains or unpicked
The golden threads from the bright tapestry.
But a rumour has got out,
Though you did your best to stifle it,
Circulates the sleeping land
Like a breeze, an encouraging whisper.
The adder stirs and tastes the air with its tongue,
The hawk on high hangs still and listening,
Bluebells carpet the woods
In Bellshill as much as in Hallaig:
The old wolf has been seen roaming the forest.

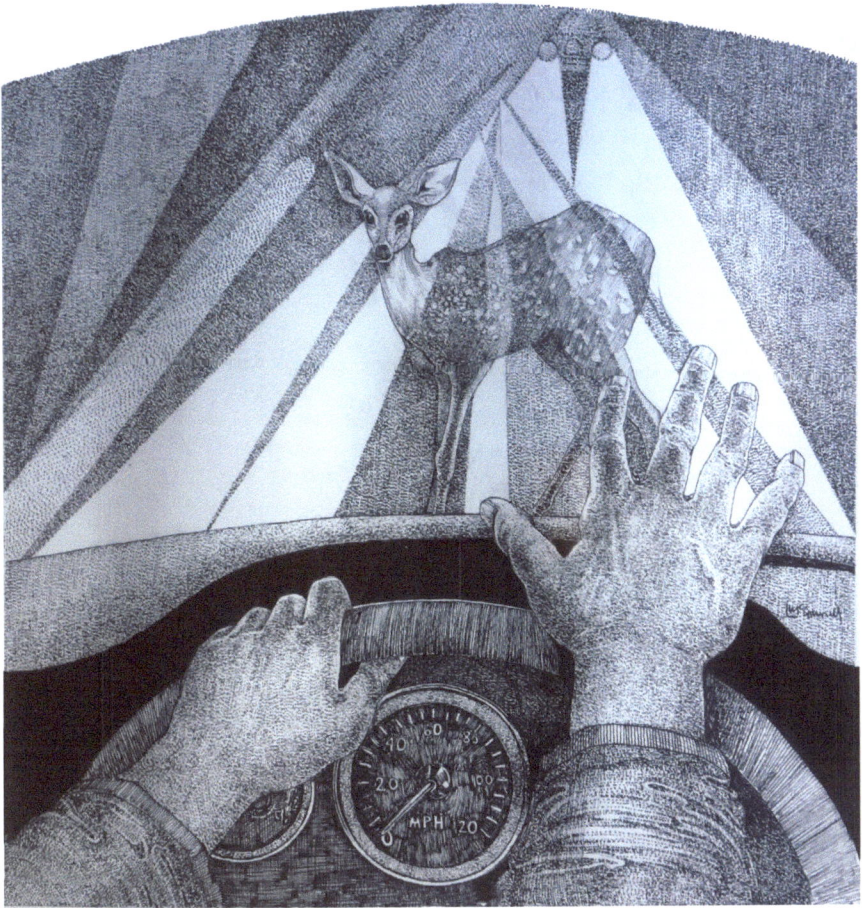

Angie

I bought the Bert Jansch Sampler
on Transatlantic, second hand in Perth.
A faded sticker dated it: 14s&5d.
Sliding the scratched vinyl from its fousty sleeve
with care I noticed the blotches of dried red wine,
was well-chuffed with this provenance.
My fancy tried to frame the first listener:
strumming along on a high action Yamaha,
struggling with those tricky DADGAD fingerings
in a student bed-sit when the meter clicked out.

A discordant note dismissed the fantasy:
it was me all along, pissed out my head,
beyond caring of spillage, blissfully unsentient
that one day I'd be dogging through racks,
ferreting with aged, shakey, liver-spotted hands
to buy back my withered vine of youth...

Extinction Rebellion

I fauldit a wittin
In a tuim plastic bottle
And flung it faur out in the weet.

"Gin ye find this gae rescue
The hetteran Warld."
The waves brocht it back tae ma feet.

Grey Heron

You augur an emaciated poetry
shredding the empty kirk of birks
named after you.
You stalk the bare wood, querulous,
in a painstaking huff, staying silent and put
in the haar-hushed gloom hall all winter,
deep in your divinations.

Even the sixpence-sized goldcrest
will back himself against the winds
in his tilt at the warm South,
but no risk taker you,
A po-faced wader of shallows,
wintering a bad job out or stretching it to
the odd away day break from standing still
to pirate suburban carp ponds.

Wheasle

Birlan his pauchled egg gallus
in plen sicht o creation
he winks tae the glaickit rabbit,
sneeteran in sel-admiration.

Or keekin his impudent face
fae the tenement o the byre waa,
gies the polis collie a sherrickan,
for abusin his richts under law .

"Dinnae fash, I've anely the len o it,"
tips his bunnet and grins tae the hens
scartin their indignation,
"I'll cry back the nicht tae explen."

Otter

Balaclavaed for special nicht operations,
he smouls ashore in the greying o the daw,
his tunic droukit, his neb dreepan,
his ration pack still wriggling in his mooth.
Croose in his quiet wey,
he rowes hisel in a kelp bathrobe,
scours oot saut draps
fae his retro seivinties feather cut,
mission accomplished.
He'll report back tae base syne disappear
intil the common five echts.
Ask the Scarf, speir the Tarrock -
alang the bar o the shoreline's
neuks and howffs, the conversation ceases.
Naebody seems tae seen him.

Ainster Herbour, Hogmanay

The daft dolphins kythed tae hansel the New Year,
heezin theirsel juist efter keek o daw,
lowpan their length tae kiss the cranreugh air,
doukan and jinkan outby the herbour waa.

First-fuitters souman the here and nou,
stravaigan the sea-road for chancie swaws,
lauchin grey cheils mang the swey and the pou
o Aul Faither Time's sleekit unnertaws.

Fushin for whillyhaas, tummelin for scags,
gaun in a glisk wi a grin hauflin-wyce,
sing land-fowk their fortune ma gallus ghaist lads -
you're ower sib tae anthropomorphise.

King Lear

Maucht raxes tae mair micht,
whiles weak's taen tae the waa:
the wolf devours the lamb
and that is aa.

Gin thon's the mint o life,
syne naethin comes o naethin -
a thraw o daith - yet Love's a lowe
for dwaiblins tae hae faith in.

Hamlet

And aye ma faither walks aheid
and grues at me as gif there was
some mishanter I've no mindit,
some funeral office that I forgot tae tent ...

Alang ghaistly ramparts o memrie,
in smaa hours corridors o wanrest,
I trauchle efter, speirin like a bairn...
he turns and glowers but bides silent.

Macbeth

Gin the nicht-gaun catogle,
mousan laichlie in its flicht,
should birl the heich-maist earn
and kill him ae daurk nicht.

Gin the flummoxed feartie maukin
that trummles amang the girss,
should daur the doverin lion
and murder him first.

Gin aa the King's proud cuddies
sae cantie, tame and douce,
should feed upon each ither,
crazy, wud-eened, crouse.

Gin the witches' slee graymaulkin
wi bluid clartin his paws,
should obey the scraighan puddock
and lowse his jaws.

Gin the Stag-King o the Glen
that roars lodged in his pluck
should abdicate his kinrick
tae some lowpan courrant buck.

 Gin aathing ranked the conter
and order kittled thrawn,
like a corbie in a blaff o wind
the world wad suin be gaun.

Oor Wullie's Intimations of Mortality

Fat Bob's like twaa ply reek, a bag o banes.
Soapy's pan breid, leavened by the big C.
Wee Eck caught Covid, nou he's weill again.
Love never gelled atween Primrose and me.

Ma disnae ken she's in a Newport Hame
Yet minds the mills, her youthheid in Lochee.
"Non-union Unionist" screived on his stane,
Pa's plantit in the Logie Cemetery.

Plumber tae tred, I'm warkin for the Broons -
The builders rin by Daphne, Joe and Hen.
I puit in hot tubs, biggin en suite rooms -
There's siller tae be made fae but and bens.

Puir Jeemie's happed in strae, Murdoch in cley.
Aa mice and men bob thrang syne spule agley.

Poet & Artist

William Hershaw: Poet, playwright, singer and musician. He is a member of the editorial board of *Lallans*. He is the founder of the folk group The Bowhill Players who perform music celebrating Fife's Coal Mining culture. In 2018 Grace Note Publications published *The Sair Road*, his Scots language version of the *Stations of the Cross* set during the 1984 Miners' Strike. His poems and songs have been widely published and recorded both in Scotland and abroad.

Les McConnell: Born in Ayrshire in 1947. He received his art education at Edinburgh College of Art in the 1960's. In 1970 he was awarded a post graduate scholarship spending part of the time in Holland. He has participated in numerous exhibitions including the Royal Scottish Academy, the Society of Scottish Artists and a one man show in Fife. The collaboration with William Hershaw started in 2017 and has proved to be a very successful partnership resulting in a number of publications and exhibitions. Working with William opened a rich seam of visual possibilities, the depth and descriptive quality of his writing make the images leap from the page. This latest work has been an exciting journey into Scotland's past.

www.ingramcontent.com/pod-product-compliance
Lightning Source LLC
LaVergne TN
LVHW010017070426
835511LV00001B/13